13250519R00055

Printed in Great Britain
by Amazon